# TIME FOR KIDS
## Nonfiction Readers

# INVENTIONS IN
## Communications

### Debra J. Housel

# Table of Contents

# Reading and Writing

Imagine firelight dancing on a cave wall.  A man dressed in a bear skin stands there.  He draws on the wall with a piece of coal to tell a story about his life.

Thousands of years later, you turn on your family's computer and send an e-mail message to your grandma.

You and the man in the bear skin are doing the same thing.  You are *communicating*.

To **communicate** is to send and receive messages.

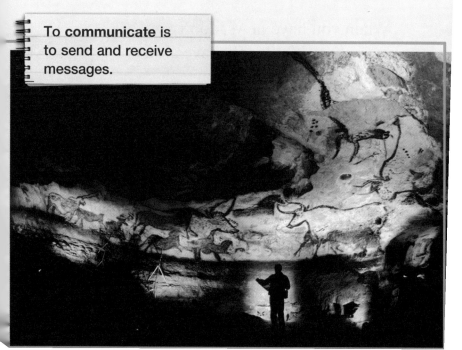

▲ cuneiform

hieroglyphs ▶

When you have news, don't you want to share it? People have always wanted to share information.

Written history begins over 5,000 years ago. Back then, words looked like drawings. They were called *cuneiforms* (kyoo-NEE-uh-forms) and *hieroglyphs* (hi-ruh-GLIFS). They were carved into stone or clay.

Later, people made ink and wrote on *scrolls* or thin pieces of animal skin.

The Chinese invented paper. With paper, more things could be written. Yet few people could read or write.

There were few books, too. Each one had to be written by hand! That could take years. Then came the printing press with movable type. Type is wood or metal letters that can be put in any order. The type was covered with ink and pressed onto paper. Many copies could be made of the same page.

## The First Paper

Paper was first made about 2,000 years ago. In those days, certain plants were soaked in water, washed, soaked some more, and beaten to a pulp with a wooden club. Then, the pulp was pressed into a mold for drying. When dry, it held together. And that was paper!

The first books were written by hand. ▼

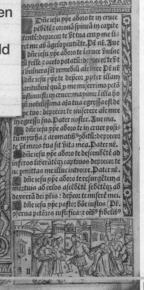

◄ Johannes Gutenberg invented the movable type printing press in 1440.

Over time more people learned to read.  Even so, only the rich owned books.

Before the 1800s, there were few public libraries in the world.  Then a man named Andrew Carnegie (CAR-nuh-gee) gave millions of dollars to build them.  He offered a world of knowledge for free.

## Carnegie

Carnegie believed that rich people should give away the money they and their families don't need.  He thought the money should be spent helping others. His donation helped to build more than 2,500 public libraries throughout the English-speaking world.

a girl using sign language ▼

## Library of Congress

The Library of Congress in Washington, D.C., is the world's largest library. There are millions of books there.  A new book is added every six seconds!

Have you ever seen raised dots next to numbers on elevator buttons? The dots are a type of writing called Braille.

As a young blind boy, Louis Braille wanted to read. At fifteen, he made a system of raised dots for letters and numbers. They can be felt and read with the fingers. In this way, blind people can read.

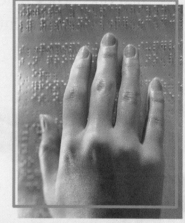

▲ The Braille system is used worldwide. It allows blind people to read.

## Sign Language

The deaf have a special language, too. They use a series of hand motions called sign language. It is a way of communicating without spoken words.

◄ The Library of Congress

Do you use gel pens?  Long before them was the ballpoint pen.  In 1935 two brothers made the first one.  They hated the ink spots fountain pens made.  They invented a pen that wouldn't spot.

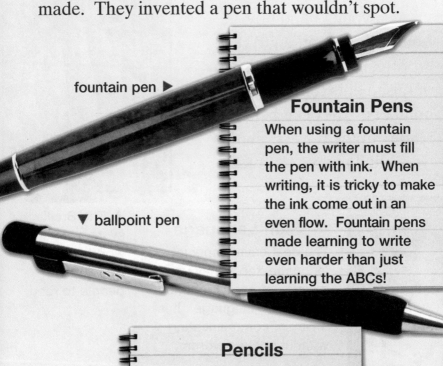

fountain pen ▶

▼ ballpoint pen

## Fountain Pens

When using a fountain pen, the writer must fill the pen with ink.  When writing, it is tricky to make the ink come out in an even flow.  Fountain pens made learning to write even harder than just learning the ABCs!

## Pencils

In 1565, the first pencil was made of wood filled with a mineral called graphite. People used pencils for at least 300 years before rubber erasers. To erase errors, they used bread chunks. Today a pencil can write 45,000 words before it is used up!

Before 1876, all writing was done by hand. Then one man changed all that. He invented the typewriter. Soon typists learned to touch type without looking at their hands. It is a very fast way to write!

▼ a very old typewriter

## QWERTY

To keep often-used keys from striking each other, the typewriter inventor laid out a keyboard set-up called QWERTY. Later keyboards were made which enabled faster typing. But since so many people knew QWERTY, the other keyboards never caught on. Just look at a computer keyboard. What letters do you read near the top left corner?

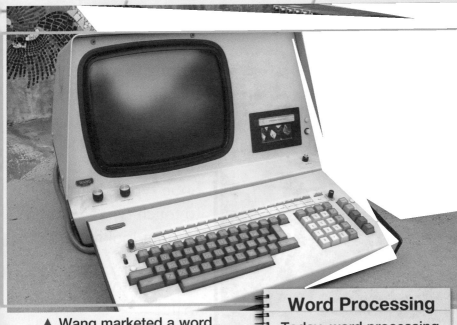

▲ Wang marketed a word processing system in 1979.

**Word Processing**
Today, word processing is done on computers.

Another big change came in 1976. The Wang *word processor* was invented. It let someone type while the words appeared on a screen. The typist could fix mistakes without starting over and then print a perfect page.

Years ago a teacher used a *ditto* to make copies of a worksheet. A ditto is a special inked paper. Copies are made by placing the ditto on a drum and rolling it against paper.

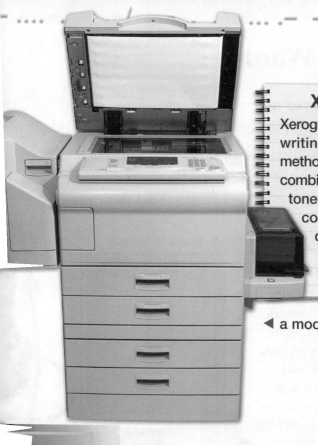

## Xerography

Xerography means "dry writing." Using this method, copy machines combine electricity with toner powder to make copies of documents.

◀ a modern copy machine

Today most teachers use copy machines. Copy machines work with *xerography* (zih-RAHG-ruh-fee). It took a long time for the inventor to make a good copy machine. But once they caught on, dittos were history!

◀ Ditto machines required special paper to make copies.

-.-. .- -. / -.-- --- ..- / .-. . .- -..

# Hearing Words

Samuel Morse made the *telegraph* in 1838. His code changed letters into tapped dashes and dots. These sounds moved through copper wires. People at the other end heard the taps. They wrote the words so others could read the message.

▼ Samuel Morse

## Morse Code

Morse's first message wasn't sent for six years after the telegraph was invented. It took that long to run the wires between cities! The first message went between Washington, D.C. and Baltimore on May 24, 1844. It read, "What hath God wrought?"

an early
telegraph
machine ▶

▼ Morse code

This sentence was written from Washington by me at the Baltimore Terminus at 8 45 min on Friday, May 24 1844, being the first transe

W h a t h a t h g

/ .. ... / .--- .-. .. - - . -. / .. -

▼ an antique telephone

**Did You Know?**

In 1956 a telephone cable was laid across the floor of the Atlantic Ocean. It lies between Canada and Scotland and is still in use today.

▲ The world's first phone call was made in 1876. Alexander Graham Bell called his assistant, Mr. Watson.

Alexander Graham Bell tried to build a machine to help deaf children speak. Instead, it became the telephone. Soon, phone lines shared telegraph poles. Phone operators sat at a big *switchboard*. They plugged wires into the switchboard to connect one person's phone to another's.

◄ using an old-style telegraph

Now many people use *cell phones*. During a call, a cell phone sends radio waves to a nearby *cell tower*. *Fiber optic cables* carry the message to a cell tower near the receiver. The second cell tower sends out radio waves to another cell phone. All of this takes just a few seconds.

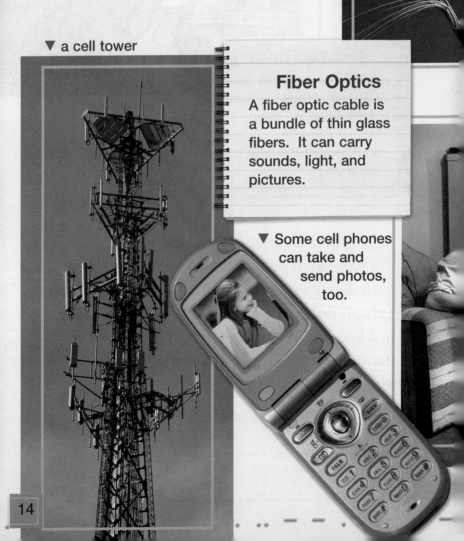

▼ a cell tower

## Fiber Optics

A fiber optic cable is a bundle of thin glass fibers. It can carry sounds, light, and pictures.

▼ Some cell phones can take and send photos, too.

By 1920, many people had radios in their homes. Radio stations broadcast things as they happened. Everyone in the family gathered around to listen to speeches, live music, and more.

Later the *transistor* (tran-ZIS-tuhr) led to small radios that people could carry.

## Recorded Music

Once the record album came out in 1948, radios began playing recorded music. By the 1960s, music came on cassette tapes, too. Compact discs, or CDs, arrived in 1982.

an old radio ▶

# Putting Sight and Sound Together

When George Eastman invented film, he wanted everyone to enjoy it. His company made the first box cameras. They were easy to use. Soon everyone was taking photos.

## Movies

In 1896, the Lumiere brothers in France made the first silent film. Since the pictures moved, they were called *movies*. Sound was added to movies by the late 1920s.

At first photos were black and white. Color came later.

## Don't Move!

The first photos took a long time to take, so people had to stay very still so the photo wouldn't be blurry.

Now people wanted moving pictures in their homes. What was the result? Television. A television works by turning signals into pictures. A coating covers the back of the TV screen. It glows when hit by electric signals.

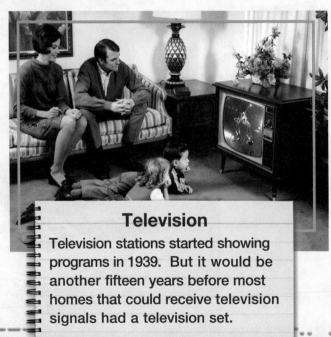

## Television

Television stations started showing programs in 1939. But it would be another fifteen years before most homes that could receive television signals had a television set.

# Communicating by Satellite

Communication *satellites* (SAT-uhl-ites) orbit Earth. They get signals from computers and cameras on one part of our planet and send them to other places on Earth. Satellites let people watch what's happening far away.

# Computers and the Internet

The first computer was so large it took up a whole room. It was run by thousands of vacuum tubes, switches, and other parts. But it was very slow.

It was built in the 1940s. But in 1959, the *microchip* was invented, and computers were changed forever. Microchips made small, personal computers possible.

The first computer was called ENIAC, the Electronic Numerical Integrator Analyzer and Computer. ▼

a variety of microchips ▶

## How Small?

Today scientists have developed computers that come from human DNA, the parts of our cells that make us who we are. They are called biological computers. They are so small that one trillion of them can fit in a drop of water!

No one set out to invent the *Internet*. The U.S. Defense Department started a computer *network* so they could receive and send messages during a war. Colleges made networks, too. Then, everybody linked their networks together. The growing network was named the Internet in 1983.

Some groups were not able to link to the Internet because of software problems. In 1990, *World Wide Web* software let all Internet programs work together. Suddenly, people could link their computers to a network that reached around the globe!

Pages on the World Wide Web are called Web sites. Each Web site has an address. To find an address, use a *search engine*. Just type what you are looking for. Within seconds the screen will show many Web sites to visit. Click on one and off you go!

▼ There are millions of websites just
   waiting for you to explore.

### Web Addresses

You can tell something about a Web site from its address. For example, if the address ends with *.com*, it is a business. When the address ends in *.gov*, it is a government site. Schools have addresses that end with *.edu*.

## Instant Messaging

With *instant messaging* you and a friend must be *online* at the same time.  Then you can write messages to each other that are read instantly.

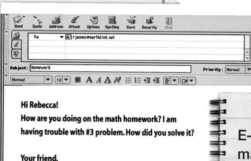

Hi Rebecca!
How are you doing on the math homework? I am having trouble with #3 problem. How did you solve it?

Your friend,
Matt

## E-mail

E-mail stands for electronic mail that is sent between computers.  You don't need a stamp for e-mail!

Have you ever sent an *e-mail* message?  If you know a person's e-mail address, you can write to him or her. Pressing the send button sends your message to a *server*.  The server holds the message until your friend retrieves it.

# Communication Inventions

These are some of the inventions that have changed communications.

| Invention | Year |
|---|---|
| ink | 2500 BC |
| paper | 105 AD |
| printing press | 1447 |
| pencil | 1565 |
| manual alphabet | 1816 |
| Braille text | 1824 |
| telegraph | 1844 |
| typewriter | 1876 |
| telephone | 1876 |
| phonograph | 1877 |
| fountain pen | 1884 |
| camera | 1888 |
| silent movie | 1896 |
| radio | 1901 |
| movie with sound | 1927 |
| television | 1929 |
| ballpoint pen | 1935 |
| television station | 1936 |
| computer (ENIAC) | 1945 |
| transistor | 1948 |
| record album | 1948 |
| copy machine | 1959 |
| microchip | 1959 |
| home/personal computer | 1975* |
| word processor | 1979 |
| Internet | 1983 |
| World Wide Web | 1990 |

*Different sources credit different people and companies with making the first personal computer.

| Inventor |
| --- |
| unknown |
| Cai Lun |
| Johannes Gutenberg |
| Konrad von Gesner |
| Thomas Hopkins |
| Louis Braille |
| Samuel Morse |
| C. Latham Sholes |
| Alexander Graham Bell |
| Thomas Edison |
| Lewis E. Waterman |
| George Eastman |
| August & Jean-Louis Lumiere |
| Nikola Tesla & Guglielmo Marconi |
| Warner Brothers |
| Vladimir Zworykin |
| Laszlo & Georg Biro |
| British Broadcasting Company (BBC) |
| University of Pennsylvania |
| Bell Telephone Laboratories |
| Columbia Records |
| Chester Carlson |
| Jack Kilby & Robert Noyce |
| Apple Computers |
| An Wang |
| U.S. Department of Defense |
| Tim Berners-Lee |

*Because the definition of personal computer differs, so does the credit for the first personal computer.*

People have been communicating throughout time. But communicating has become faster and easier in the last 100 years. What do you think the next big invention in communication might be?

# Glossary

**Braille**   a system of raised dots that forms text, allowing the blind to read

**cell phone**   a portable phone that works by radio waves; short for cellular telephone

**cell tower**   a tower with many antennas which sends and receives radio waves from cellphones

**communication**   sharing information through reading, writing, speaking, listening and watching

**cuneiform**   picture-based writing that was carved into clay tablets by writers long, long ago

**Ditto**   the name of an inked paper used to make copies

**e-mail**   electronic message sent between linked computers; short for "electronic mail"

**fiber optic cable**   a bundle of thin glass fibers that carry information in the form of light energy

**hieroglyphics**   pictures and symbols used by ancient Egyptians to stand for sounds and objects

**instant messaging**   typing and receiving messages over the Internet in real time (instantly)

**Internet**   a worldwide system of linked computer networks

**microchip**   a small, thin piece of silicon (a natural substance found in the earth) with electronic circuits on it, used in computers

**network**   a group of things connected to each other over the network

**online**   connected to the Internet

**satellite**   an object that orbits the Earth

**scroll**   a piece of parchment (a kind of paper) with writing on it that rolls up into the shape of a tube

**search engine**   software that looks through the World Wide Web for requested information

**server**   the computer that lets files pass between computers in the network

**switchboard**   the control board for connecting the lines of a telephone system

**telegraph**   an electronic machine that sends signals through wires by using a series of taps

**transistor**   a tiny electronic piece that controls the flow of electric currents; short for "transfer resistance"

**word processor**   a machine or computer program used to type, edit, store, and print documents

**World Wide Web**   software that allows computers to link to the Internet

**xerography**   the method by which copy machines combine electricity with toner (a type of printing ink) in order to copy documents

# Index